DESCENDING INTO WAR, DESCENDING INTO CONTEMPT

Spiritual sharing about human behavior that is misunderstood

*Book Seven of the
Existence-Me Elevated Living Series*

Renee Rothberg

Descending into War, Descending into Contempt

www.energy-guidance-complete.com

ISBN 978-1973766780

Cover design by Valentina Gribovska
Edited by Tina Ornstein
Printed by CreateSpace, an Amazon.com company
Available on Kindle and other devices

Other books by the author

Existence-Me Elevated Living book series:

The Gift of Intuitive, Dedicated Comfort

Pond a Connected Existence

Oneself—Living

Vitality!

Awaiting Light—Understanding the Development of the Soul

Signals that Inspire and Intertwine—The Fifth Component of Health

Inspirational:

Exploring Energy Guidance Complete, My Journey

Contracts for an Exemplary Life

Samba 'til the End—Experiencing Well-Being in the Later Years

Play:

Zoo Conversations—Giving Voices to the Animals

Poetry:

Unfolding—A Collection of Wisdom Poetry

Connection—A Collection of Wisdom Poetry

Faith— A Wisdom Poem Sharing Spiritual Connection

Growth—A Collection of Wisdom Poetry

CONTENTS

INTRODUCTION

D ESCENT into war is the visible manifestation of the struggles felt by men. Within a man are powerful forces of fearlessness and faithfulness. These forces push towards action when the family or loved society is threatened or harmed. Deep, devoted love can lead to horrific acts that are delivered in order to protect loved ones or revenge their harm.

This ability to inflict destruction in order to protect can be misunderstood, and can then be used for the sake of the harm. Internal rage can develop unchecked, which erupts into violence or contemptuous behavior. The violent behavior is unnatural, but it feeds on natural emotions and past experiences.

War is always a descent. It is never a positive choice. Contempt, too, is always a descent. It brings only negativity and misguided thinking and actions.

Contempt summons from a place within: a negative place that is created after birth, not part of the original emotions and the opposite of natural human expression. It materializes when feelings of disappointment, envy, superiority, rejection, and resentment combine to disturb thinking and the building of opinions. Contempt has no societal value. It destroys relationships and negotiations.

Contempt—that which stays unspoken and that which erupts into action—when allowed to mix with laws, regulations, and edicts, putrefies daily comings-and-goings and deliberations for future legislation. The members of society who create legislation that sanctions contempt and determine to continue contemptible frameworks for their society, lower their society's true potential.

The mix of disappointment, envy, rejection, resentment, and superior behavior permeates people's actions and derails them from living contentedly. Without contented living, the interactions between people are blinded by misconceptions and prejudices. Contented living is impossible when contempt is felt for others. Negativity echoes loudly, reverberating from generation to generation, creating chaos and destroying opportunities.

Descending into War, Descending into Contempt, the last book in the Existence-Me Elevated Living book series, is presented to us from Spirit for loving reasons. All the wisdom presented in the book series shows love from Spirit in the information that is shared with us. Each word has been deciphered by me, but the words belong to Spirit. The sharing is help for us to create a contempt-free world.

The ascent to cooperation feels difficult, but it is the optimal goal. Partnering with Spirit to create wise living is available. Read the books and create soulful, balanced lives!

CONTEMPT MULTIPLYING INTO CONFLICT

CONFLICT has many sources of support. The sources feed conflict when they are elevated beyond control. Each conflict source contributes to contemptuous behavior or to deliberate indifference. Each conflict has its specific sources and unique circumstances. Nonetheless, there are similarities among conflicts.

Contempt is built through feelings of superiority, feelings of inequity, feelings of disappointment, and feelings of emasculation. Each of these destructive feelings will be explored and their contributions to conflict considered.

Feelings of Superiority

The feeling of superiority is a strange phenomenon. All people are similar, and yet, there are some who consider themselves superior. These people believe that race membership, financial status, gender affiliation, nationality, religion, and/or education entitle them to raised social status. Physical attractiveness, athletic prowess, and fashion taste are other factors in people acting superior.

Superiority by Nationality

Superiority by nationality is the viewing of other nationalities in a condescending way. Feeling better than everyone who lives outside one's own country is a sense of superiority that is confrontational behavior and enemy building.

Geographical reality creates differences among countries, because some countries are situated with enviable conditions and resources that inspire jealousy or resentment. A country possessing enviable conditions and resources often maintains citizens who feel entitled to their reality and are possessive of it. Adjacent countries may have conditions and resources that are also deserving of pride, but the other country's richness seems desirous, and so, the citizens of the adjacent countries may feel resentful or covetous. The clash of entitlement and resentment can lead to rivalries, racism, and wars.

Superiority by nationality describes relationships among countries, but it can also describe relationships among areas within a country, towns within a province, neighborhoods within a city, and loyalty to schools or universities. At each level, the location, historical development, and geographical reality affect how citizens see their environment and the environments of those who inhabit rival territories. Those who feel they have more behave differently from those who feel deprived. Each side can feel superior and relate to the other as less than them. The feelings of superiority at the local and inner-country levels can lead to rivalries, treachery, and self-destruction.

Superiority Because of Gender

Superiority by consideration of one's sex as better creates conflict within society at the family level, within neighborhoods and religions, and in nations. Gender superiority is often inculcated from an early age, so that belief in one's gender superiority is very deep.

Contempt towards "inferiors" develops more easily in those with a sense of gender superiority.

Superiority Learned from Childhood

Superiority is a learned behavior. A child is self-interested, because he has his own concerns that consume his attention. This behavior is inborn. The child focuses on himself, not from a sense of superiority, but from the need to survive.

The child encounters others with curiosity, joy, and fear. When a caregiver over-elevates the child's sense of himself, encounters with others have lessened curiosity, joy, and fear and more expectations of subservience (by the others).

Internal sense of superiority develops from a young age and can be based on gender, race, physical appearance, and attitude. Later come superiority based on religion, social standing, intelligence, and financial status. Subservient behavior by others and athletic prowess can increase the sense of superiority.

Superiority Because of Religion

Many paths of elevation are available and desirable for reaching connection with God. Solitary prayer unites divinity with creation for the moments the connection is true. Prayer in groups unites divinity with creation for elevated connection when the connection is sincere. Both solitary prayer and grouped prayer are paths to God.

Grouped prayers, which are developed into set pronouncements with set movements, remove creativity in building spiritual connection, but encourage human connection. Repetition of "scripts" and routine observances enable feelings of human connection that transcend death. This connection can bind the living with the dead who preceded them, and bind the living with future generations.

Grouped prayer connects the people who accept the group's observances and concept of divinity. Acceptance offers approach to God, scripts that guide the approach, and visions to ponder Almighty: the majestic energy that connects all.

Sincere dedication to life lived with awareness of connection to God is realistic. The connection focuses and elevates daily living.

Dedication to the grouped approach to God—to the religion—is dedication missing the meaning. Religion is an accessway for connecting to God; it is not the destination. Elevating the religion, rather than the divine connection, disconnects people from

God. Religions are approaches, they are not possessions to be coveted or aggrandized. They do not need to be compared or debated.

Superiority is not a word to describe a religion. **No religion that is based on the connection with God is better than any other.** Feeling superior because of religious affiliation lessens the beauty of the religion.

Religious superiority is the most destructive belief of all. No religious group has closer connection to God than any other. **No group!**

Superiority Because of Race

Condescension because of race is irrational. Belittling others because of race is weak. Generalizing about race is uninformed. Thinking disparaging thoughts about other races is contemptuous.

Superiority because of the foolish thinking that race has influence on value is deluded. No race is superior to any other. Race is variations of people. No more, no less.

Superiority in Societies

Feeling superior can be intricate, based on all the causes set out above, or it can be single-cause—no matter, the sense of superiority is there. It affects all relationships and all interactions.

Societal sense of superiority, like individual sense of superiority, is learned. The entire society can feel superior, as in an overinflated opinion of race or nationality, or it can be bestowed upon members of society who are treated "better" because of gender, physical appearance, financial power, athletic prowess, and other factors like fashion taste or musical/artistic abilities.

Superiority infuses society with discontent and entitlement. Superiority brings envy and distancing. Each individual builds the societal sense of superiority with internal feelings of being better than others, or by accepting the societal definitions of superior race or gender, or having subservient expectations.

The sense of superiority is distancing and clouds judgment when interacting with others. The sense of superiority tarnishes dialogue and creates contempt. As people distance, misjudge and condescend, they define a society that is uncaring and disconnected. Such a society cannot nurture its members or provide empathy.

Societal superiority affects external events. For example, natural disasters that would be handled by the affected group in a communal manner descend into further disaster because of conflicts among the group members. The more ingrained the feelings of superiority, the less the desire to help others. Disaster relief that should be inclusive is not. Those with more, be it real or perceived, dismiss the troubles of the people whom they disdain. Contempt thwarts relief efforts and distances people further.

When combined with the other causes of contempt, the sense of superiority feeds conflicts among families, communities, regions, and nations. The sense of superiority is very insidious.

Feelings of Inequity

Fairness is elusive. Nature is wide in its distribution of resources, and fairness is unrelated. Difference is the key. Nature is about differences infinitely dispersed. No two are quite the same.

Differences are physical and intangible. Within the physical manifestations are nuances and subtleties. Within the intangible characteristics are emotional ranges, instinctive differences, intellectual capacities, awareness of natural order, and survival positioning.

The rhythms in nature are the providers of fairness. As the days roll one into another and the seasons instill movement of time, the living experience the rhythms together. From the tiniest elements to complex humans, all feel the rhythms. Fairness is in the togetherness.

In each person are a call for togetherness and a call for investment. The investment requires preserving self-interest and desiring closeness given by others. Innate awareness and activation of attachment reactions drive each person to connect and protect.

Morés and group behaviors affect the innate attachment reactions and introduce skewed expectations for societal position, close attachments, and intuitive evaluations. The skewed thinking is learned and ingrained, and is then reflected in thinking and behaviors.

Within individual family units and communal groups, relationships develop and end. The larger units—towns, subdivisions, and areas connected by loyalties—contain the family units and communal groups, and they change opportunities for attachments. Each relationship and attachment presents hopes, expectations, and reactions. Each relationship and attachment has the possibilities of closeness and skewed evaluation. Each relationship and attachment reflects ingrained thinking and natural responses. Innate and learned behaviors intertwine.

The natural inclination is to expect differences in others. The learned misinterpretation is to expect fairness. Just as superiority is learned and inculcated in people, so too is the expectation of fairness.

Fairness is often expected in everything: fairness in distribution of attention in relationships, fairness in access to solutions, fairness in competitions, fairness in natural conditions (weather and resources), and fairness in efforts towards well-being.

Parents are expected to treat their children "fairly". The price charged for a service is expected to be "fair". Less fairness is expected in societies where wealth is unethically distributed. Fairness is not expected, nor is it hoped for, when governing forces repress some. This effect is created in societies that support slavery, religious self-righteousness, and caste systems. Less fairness is also expected in societies that ennoble power, buildings, or might.

Conflict is aroused when inequality becomes too difficult to maintain, or when those with "less" force change.

Within a family, conflict erupts over the inability to be fair. Family members perceive treatment from different vantage points, and inequality seethes in the relationships. The feelings of inequity can lead to divorce, estrangement, miscommunication, or self-harm. Feelings of inequity are family-fracturing.

Within schools, feelings of inequity can abound. Administrators who establish blatant inequality among staff, drive mistrust and jealousy into the school. School board members sometimes have their positions because of unethically distributed wealth, and they force inequity through their voting rights. Students increase feelings of inequity when they have superiority in their upbringing. Classrooms, which are headed by teachers who allow their personal preferences for students to affect their work, are places where conflict can breed.

Within businesses, inequity naturally exists because of ownership privileges (although mistreatment of employees should not be condoned).

Departmental inequity that is encouraged by upper management is mismanagement. Departmental inequity that is created within departments is pernicious.

Negotiations between businesses exude self-interest. Focus on own-ness is natural and is expected. In negotiations in which businesses use unethical tactics or withhold information, the offending side brings inequity into the negotiations. The results will be distancing and will be destabilizing to society. The results will extend beyond the individual businesses negotiating.

Feelings of inequity surface in citizens of countries beset by government officials who covet the imagined riches of other countries. Imagined, for reality is fraught with hardships unseen. When the governing officials have instilled in their citizens feelings of covetousness and inequity, the view towards other countries will be skewed. Skewed appreciation of one's own reality can lead to conflicts with those imagined to have a more desirable reality. The conflicts can lead to injustices and armed conflict.

Feelings of Disappointment

Disappointment is a feeling that afflicts from an early age, and no one is immune from its appearance. The growth process is accelerated when people work through feelings of disappointment.

It is not a negative emotion when it is a catalyst for appreciation and adaptation.

Sometimes, disappointment is an accelerator of despair. Disappointment with despair is more difficult to overcome, but when they have been faced and handled, the growth process continues. When they are not handled, the disappointment can underlie future responses to ordinary happenings. When despair is mixed with feelings of inequity and with inaction to change the situation, the feelings of disappointment can increase the likelihood of conflicts.

Disappointment on its own lowers vigor. When disappointment is accompanied by feelings of inequity, of violation, or of injury, desire for revenge or sabotage can foment.

Disappointment at the group level (two or more people), which comes from the feeling of having received unfair treatment, waits for a trigger that will either direct towards dismissal of the urge to act (restraint) or release restraint towards action (positive or negative). The release of restraint can unite group members or create disunity, because each group member experiences disappointment differently.

Disappointment can also be an accelerator of demoralization. When this situation happens, the strength of disappointment overcomes surety of self and challenges courage. Courage is needed when envisioning possible disasters and when immersed in challenging feats. Disappointment dampens courage, and then when courage is needed, it (courage) is less commanding.

The other contributors to conflict—feelings of superiority, feelings of inequity, and feelings of emasculation—are intensified when disappointment accelerates feelings of despair or demoralization. Disappointment can be a strong emotion, and it intensifies feelings of contempt and the possibility of conflict.

Feelings of Emasculation

Relationships require validation of all the participants. The relationships, whether between two people or many nations, establish frameworks in which people can create their lives. Validation comes from feeling secure in the relationships.

The feeling of security is very important to men and women. It enables them to work towards common goals—goals that fulfill expectations and aspirations. When security is lacking in relationships, people experience conflict. They can also experience instability, fear, and abandonment. Insecurity in relationships, no matter the size of the relationships—in a marriage, in a business partnership, or in negotiations with comparably situated people (negotiations between businesses, organizations, or nations)—affects feelings particular to men.

Men who feel powerful in negotiations in which the other side(s) feels powerless, temporarily feel satisfied, but experience insecurity due to recognition that the "winning" brings with it the mistrust of the other side(s). For the "powerful", the sense of domination creates an atmosphere of never-ending control that must be maintained; otherwise, winning will be lost, and this responsibility to be powerful emasculates them through self-inflicted castigation. Winning appears to be the goal, but in actuality, winning places the powerful in a prison of never-ending doubts and posturing.

Men who feel powerless in negotiations develop protective shells around themselves that allow them to acquiesce or rationalize their inability to prevail. These shells are helpful in handling loss, but they don't alleviate feelings of emasculation. The feelings of emasculation can cause withdrawal, depresssion, and desire for revenge.

Powerlessness in negotiations destabilizes society, because all those affected are surrounded by its effects on the men. Whether the powerlessness produces withdrawal, depression, or desire for revenge, these feelings simmer inside and influence actions. Powerlessness can create large reprisals when men who desire revenge group together and allow the revenge rallying call to determine their actions. The need for revenge is strong for men.

Men who feel rejected, whether by society or by individual society members, react. Their reactions are self-critical, or incite self-examination, or inspire hatred, or distance them from others. The reactions to self-criticism because of rejection can differ from rejection to rejection, depending on the frequency of rejections and the support network of the man being rejected.

When the reactions to rejection are bewilderment and hurt, the reactions can intimidate some men and cause them to reduce connections to the hurtful sources of rejection. Bewilderment and hurt can also cause some men to examine social interactions, reassess the rejections, and use the rejections as lessons in life. Learning from rejection restores confident participation in relationships.

When the reactions to rejection are retreat and blame, men and women suffer. Men suffer more if they feel emasculated by the rejection. Feelings of reduced dignity or feelings of wronging one's honor impact men differently, depending on character strength, past abuse from others, and feelings of superiority. The influences of societal expectations, judgment-altering catalysts (drugs [legal or illegal], alcohol, or overwhelming experiences of belittlement), or scruples sway a man towards—or away from—negative actions that trespass on others.

The sway towards harming others, be they people, animals, property or family, pushes actions that damage the others. The force of the sway towards harming others is strong, and it engulfs a man and takes over his reasoning capabilities. The strength of the force governs thoughts and over-whelms bodily weakness or intervention. The emasculated sense of self that has allowed the strength of the force towards negative action to take control over thoughts and justifies the feelings of emasculation, enables men to rape, over-damage, abuse, and ruin others.

The nature of men is NOT to do these things; the nature of destroyed sense of self creates the fantasy that men do these things. Men, no matter their testosterone, are NOT meant to harm; they are meant to create. Creating and building and exploring and challenging the body and mind are natural outlets for testosterone-driven men. Pillaging and abusing and oppressing and grandiosizing are the fantasies of men with destroyed sense of self.

The mix of rejection with feelings of superiority and disappointment is a powerful mix for contempt. Comfort in connections prevents emasculated thinking. Insecurity in relationships brings it forth.

The Equation of Conflict

The possibility of conflict floats. It floats on the interactions of people, and changes course as posturing and understanding moves back and forth.

Each conflict has its variables and relations. They change over time and resolve. Separate from some conflicts is humility. Without humility, con-flicts fester and widen. Resolution requires drastic changes in environmental conditions, being united by a common goal, or magnanimous acts of generosity.

The breadth of conflict is dimensional. Small conflicts between a few people are possible. Each conflict has its participants and its issues. The issues are dimensional too, because each participant's view of the issues is different. Resolving "small" conflicts can be as difficult as resolving larger ones. The smallness is relative and depends on the willingness of the participants to negotiate the conflict.

Dimensional too are the emotional states of each conflict participant. Emotional feelings fluctuate and are influenced by the destructive feelings that incite contemptuous eruptions. Conflict resolution is influenced by emotions that play leading roles in resolution outcome.

The equation of conflict and conflict resolution is indiscriminate. Conflict isn't present when people want the amount that quenches their natural hungers. It isn't present when people objectively assess their needs and notice the needs of others. But, when people covet or want more than they need, the equation begins to form, and it pulls in the people who create the conflict and all others who directly participate or indirectly become involved.

The equation of conflict is built into some social networks, such as in religions and cultures. The religions and cultures that diminish the status of the "other" codify conflict, which then forces perpetual conflict on its members and believers. Built-in conflict negates spiritual ascension so that practitioners of conflict-ridden religions and members of conflict-encouraged societies cannot have spiritual access—no matter how much they desire it. Only by rejecting the superiority espoused by their religion or social group can they achieve spiritual ascension.

The sources and circumstances of conflict—so many and so easily started! A person could admit defeat in trying to resolve conflict. Accepting conflict as being beyond change is short-sighted. Staying in continuous conflict is actually more effort than working to harmoniously coexist.

Sources of conflict pervade the human condition and they encourage destruction or repair, depending on each person's viewpoint. Repair is the better choice.

THE DESIRE FOR POWER

"I hope our wisdom will grow with our
power, and teach us, that the less we use
our power the greater it will be."

IN this quote by Tom Jefferson, power is in front
of us, to be used when needed, with awareness of
its effects and with awareness of its dangers. Awareness is the important factor for power, because its
intoxicating nature is addictive.

The availability of power is elusive; it seems to
be permanent when it is in one's possession, yet it
can fail when the power is assumed to be a right.
Power depends upon feelings of entitlement, ability
to speak authoritatively, physical features, self-
centeredness, and desire for control. When all that
one wants is one's own satisfaction, power becomes
addictively desired, and the feelings of entitlement
and desire for control silence the sense of
compassion. Without compassion, the desire for
power becomes personal. It becomes a character
trait that is overly defining. When power ceases, the
person is left bereft of identity and control.

Having power for the sake of power is unwise.
The power loses its focus and misdirects actions
that then bring lessened potential. Power is meant to
be used for creative endeavors, not for physical
dominance or emotional manipulation. Taking the
power, misdirecting it, and desiring its pull causes

the power-hungry person to act contemptuously. The behavior brings combative reactions into relationships and negotiations. The more the power is used needlessly, the less reliance on wisdom occurs.

Greater are the actions that spring from observation and wisdom than are the actions that push from self-importance and foolhardiness.

DREADING EVENTS

T HE stage before experiencing calamity is filled with hope, anxiety, and fear. Fear fills the lungs and shortens the breath. Anxiety flows through the blood and causes sleeplessness or hysteria. Hope is in the thoughts that the dreaded event will prove less dreadful than anticipated.

Shortening of the breath combined with sleeplessness can cause a weakened immune system, which can lead to sudden illness and incapacitation. Shortening of the breath combined with hysteria can cause behavior that is societally unacceptable, but is condoned at the moment. Shortening of the breath combined with sleeplessness and hysteria weakens the body's ability to rationally process information so that violent or retrogressive actions can occur.

These changes apply to men and women; however, societal morés influence the extent of the changes. Children descend less quickly into the consequences of shortened breath, sleeplessness, and hysteria; although they may experience hope, anxiety, and fear acutely. A person's attitude also influences the impact of hope, anxiety, and fear.

Anticipation of the calamity to come affects the spirit, undisputably. The stronger a person's sense of connection to spiritual belief, the stronger the control of emotions and the less the sinking into anxiety and fear. The connection doesn't prevent anxiety and fear from appearing, but the sense of support that comes from spiritual connection provides strength in self-conviction and self-dependence. The connection must be sincere to have the strengthening effects.

Calamities are different due to the circumstances in which they happen. A government-sanctioned purge has positive and negative effects on the inhabitants, depending on loyalties and societal standing. Supporters may be fearful, yet joyous, and those who resist may be hopeful, yet afraid. Rebellious uprisings, like government-sanctioned purges, have positive and negative effects. They embolden some and terrify others. Individual attackers, such as serial killers, frighten all because the targets are less clear and the locations seem random. Revenge seekers bring calamity that is frightening and demurring, because the victims can be anyone in any part of society. Honor killings come under the category of revenge seeking.

Fear, a natural emotion, is intensified by calamities that are real or anticipated. Anticipating violence can cause similar emotional distress as experiencing it. Experiencing violence creates altered behavior that invades subsequent actions. Experiencing violence also teaches forceful reactivity that can be released on others in the future.

When intense hatred has been experienced, the experience can be internalized and then used against others. When intense hatred is witnessed but not personally experienced, the demonstrations of intense hatred towards others may be digested un-consciously and then be displayed towards others (towards those displaying the hatred or those receiving it) in the future.

Intense hatred is an emotion that propels towards action or retreat. Either of these reactions causes internal turbulence, so that health can be compromised if the reactions are too extreme. After a calamity, intense hatred requires release so that people can handle the altered circumstances.

Calamities that become long-term evolve into ways of life. They push people to change routines and priorities, but they are less anxiety- and fear-causing. Depending on age, health and attitude, each person reacts to the changed reality by seeing beyond the new situations or pushing against them. Life situations are ever-evolving, and the nature of people is to adapt and learn new rhythms. Refusing to adapt is not human nature.

The stage before experiencing calamity is dif-ficult to endure. It is not a time for judgment of others nor high expectations. It is a time to offer help and provisions. Calamity is a change, megacos-mically or societally created, that occurs as a matter of course. To consider it rare is unrealistic. The more that people accept calamity's place in life, the more they can weather the storms and upheavals.

PREPARING FOR THE FIGHT

SIMILARITIES exist in gearing up for battles. There are physical preparations and mental conversations. Smaller battles require the same preparations as larger battles, if the stakes are crucial to either side.

In ongoing conflicts, preparation is muted by the need for constant engagement. These conflicts usually experience reduced physical and mental preparations. For fighters in from the beginning, the training and encouragement they received before feeling the endlessness of the conflict can sustain until it ends, if they believe in the cause. Fighters who enter midway, whether or not they receive preparations that rev them, experience the relief of the in-from-the-beginning fighters, and that welcome gives them a sense of purpose, or a sense of hopelessness, from the moment they arrive.

Involvement of commanders in the fighting is not the main motivator for engaging in the activity of death. The motivators are revenge, duty, and devotion to the cause. Commanders can rouse fervor, but even if they are absent, the fighters immerse themselves in the iniquities.

Fighters who are in it for financial reward or excitement have less motivation to wholeheartedly commit themselves to dying. For them, a commander's presence influences performance.

Fighters who are forced to fight, those who have been brought in against their will, also require commander presence to engage in indignations.

When judgment-altering substances are used in "motivating" fighters (drugs [legal or illegal] or alcohol), brutality increases in the activity of death. For the fighters who live past their participation in brutality, whether or not they were given mind-altering substances, nightmares and visualizations will plague them in the current life <u>and</u> in the next life to come. (Nightmares and visualizations of blood-filled scenes plague all who participate in brutality that is excessive—even for those who only followed orders.)

Circumstances often influence the age of those fighting. Organized induction of fighters or the rise of an armed conflict create fighters of set ages. In these circumstances, age affects training and performance of responsibilities. Vigilantes, who gather their fighters through force or brainwashing, usually take children and very angry people so that they can mold them. When fighters join forces for financial gain, they usually do so to support a family, and are of varied ages.

Preparing for the fight uses cleverness, wits, and intuition. These things cannot overcome massive weaponry, but they are helpful in struggles where strategy is needed. Preparing for the fight when exhaustion has set in, leads to mistakes and lack of confidence by the fighters.

No matter the preparations, though, the moments of meeting to kill are valueless.

27

FEROCITY

THE viciousness that conflict enables buries humanity in quicksand. It pulls all down down, thinning the resources to stop the expectation that ferocity and viciousness are normal behaviors.

Ferocity is an innate quality in people—in all people, but it is usually contained. When ferocity is allowed to take hold, the results are often tragic.

Unkindness is not an innate quality; it is learned. Children learn it from caregivers and people who affect their lives when they are young. If unkindness is doused on people, it drenches but does not pass into the behavior, unless the unkindness is consistently administered or is traumatically experienced. Unkindness that has become part of a person opens the person to release ferocity.

Uncontrollable hatred is also not an innate quality, but it is felt when it has been experienced or when it is lived by example. In other words, children who experience uncontrollable hatred directed at them may internalize it and use it against themselves or others, or children who see and hear demonstrations of uncontrollable hatred towards other people may unconsciously digest the hatred towards others and display it in the future. When uncontrollable hatred is felt and unkindness has been learned, ferocity develops.

Throughout history, people have viciously hurt other people. The cycle of ferocity does not change, because people continue to teach unkindness and hatred.

News stories focus on salacious and hurtful events so that people become inured to vicious and degrading actions. Books and movies describe loathsome and reprehensible characters, because people have become conditioned to see them as "entertainment".

Ferocity can be controlled, but it requires conviction, understanding, declaration (public statements), patience, vigilance, kindness, and action by participants and sideliners so that the ferocity remains inactive. Conviction is the solution to ferocity—conviction that ferocity can be controlled and neutralized.

CASUALTIES OF RESENTMENT

RESENTMENT is felt throughout the presence of conflict. Conflict naturally arouses the feelings of resentment, and it feeds the feelings, even after the conflict has resolved or disintegrated. Feelings of resentment infect relationships, self-esteem, and perceptions of society.

The casualties of resentment are many. Some of them are listed here:

- Stubbornness in negotiations

- Aggressive speech

- Feelings of emasculation

- Acceleration of feelings of despair

- Hurtful actions

- Armed confrontations

- Mistreatment of children

- Inability to protect children

- Fractured relationships

- Covetous view of one's own possessions

- Annoyance at the daily interactions with others, even when the interactions are kind

- Conflict and ill will towards segments of the population

- Lowered performance of work

- Envy of friends and close people (family, coworkers, etc.)

- Rejection of society

- Escape through numbing substances

- Investment in destructive thoughts and actions

Resentment casualties hurt. They damage others in many ways and damage the resentful ones with each resentful feeling. Resentment brings on foolish decisions, failed agreements, and pain. The effects of resentment are wide and lasting, and they destroy. From individuals to nations, resentment fosters distancing and grief.

When resentment is felt, the best solution is acknowledgement of the feelings and openness to exploration of solutions. Letting resentment fester is the wrong approach. The right approach is acknowledging resentful feelings, and then evaluating them and rectifying the thinking or the situation.

CAPITAL PUNISHMENT

C APITAL punishment is a payment that should never be extracted. No matter what another person did, capital punishment is not for people to use. Death that is deliberately meted out is improper for people to do. It creates imbalance in the people who cause it to happen—in the judges, in the juries, in the officials overseeing the event, and in the general populace.

Capital punishment has emotional side effects for the people who administer it, not for the people who receive it. Yes, those who die because of capital punishment have fears and other emotions. The side effects they don't feel are indifference, hardening, and stonyheartedness. Yes, they may have been indifferent, hardened or stonyhearted, which allowed them to commit offenses deemed worthy of death, but their mental state before execution contracts.

The feelings of the people who participate in government-sanctioned executions, from the people who administer the deaths to the people who voted for its use, are indifferent to the enormity of purposefully administered death, are hardened to changes that have happened to them because of their indifference, and have become stonyhearted—desensitized, remorseless, and indurate. The full extent of capital punishment effects are not understood, but they are wide and rippling.

Judging others is appropriate. Confining some who cannot control their misanthropic behavior is prudent. Insisting upon restitution is instructional. Bringing society towards helping the offenders before they hurt others is wise. Allowing capital punishment is misguided.

FACING DEATH

IN the struggles of conflict, death is a possible outcome.

A struggle in a family can lead to volatile emotions that result in death. A struggle between competitors can render death when the competition matters too much. Struggles because of desire for wealth or power have many negative effects, and death is in the possible realm of actions considered.

Death is meted out regularly when society is structured to suspect its inhabitants. In these cases, the conflict is codified—*de jure* or *de facto*—in both oppressive regimes and in proud nations.

Between countries, death can be a nationalistic duty when wars erupt. Deaths due to defending one's country are mourned but elevated; deaths due to betraying one's country are approved and applauded. In both cases, the deaths are the end of living. Is it good to die for one's country? The answer depends on what is left behind.

Facing death. Facing death when death is imminent—not from natural causes, but from enemy fire or enemy hands—is a moment of emptiness. The thoughts begin to run out and the body gives way. When nothing can be done to prevent the imminent death, the body freezes and starts the process of soul separation. In a natural death, the soul separates after the death occurs. In a precipitous death, the soul begins to separate when the person gives way to the death about to occur. The soul is separated so that the body dies with less anguish.

Facing death. For some, not a fear at all. For others, a motivator to grovel. The fear of death bridles no other animals except humans.

The fear, at the point when life declines into death, is wrapped and protected in ethereal love. The fear has assistance to open the soul to move on. Fear of death becomes no more.

REMODELING REALITY

CHANGING reality di-verges (di, two; verger, to incline [to bend forward or prompt to do something]) the future. The making of the future accompanies every action and every interaction that occurs. The future is constantly changing.

Objectification enables treatment of others to be inhumane. Whether the others are hated or not, inhumane treatment causes a future that is inclined towards indignations. Inhumane treatment and continued objectification of people and animals spiral into societal living that is abhorrent.

Human nature, just like the nature of each animal group, is partially unchangeable and partially controlled by internal governance. Humans live within the boundaries of their physiology and their capacities for thought. The range of boundaries and capacities is genetically, geographically, and companion-personality influenced (by parents, siblings, caregivers, and peers). In addition, the range is influenced by societal and historical frameworks. Modern influences on the range are technology, pharmacology, and rootlessness.

Hormonal influences have overall input into human behavior. The hormones, especially the sex hormones, direct the eyes, and the drive, and the desires. Choices made because of hormonal insistence are confident temporarily, while the immersion in the hormonal actions capture reason. Hormonal influences affect the future in the choices to allow them to determine actions.

Divergence of possible consequences from choices and actions! Divergence shows the future what could have been in the past. Divergence thought is shown in statements of "If only". "If only they had chosen to…" "If only the school officials had…" "If only…" If onlys are reflections on the past, but they can be used in the present to create a future that is harmonious. The current acceptance of unkindness as behavior that is part of human nature is changeable. Unkindness is not built in, and it can be softened by actions that change the future.

Men and women have hormonal forces that open them to unkind actions. Masculine and feminine unkindness can be similar, but masculine unkindness can be more destructive. The phenomenon of emasculation is the basis of horrendous destruction, as described in "Feelings of Emasculation" on pp. 14–17. Masculine submersion into the depths of destruction is the cause of crises and conflicts throughout the world. The future is often molded on the aspirations and descent of men. Women have secondary roles in most of the conflicts, because of societal and internal reasons. The future has less negativity because of women.

Conflicts can be changed into compromises and détente when the desire to coexist is nurtured. Many paths are angled towards coexistence, but these coexistence paths depend upon determination and participation to succeed.

Here is a coexistence path that understands the physical and hormonal needs of men. It requires the participation of boys and men in all stations of society. This path recognizes the energy that is generated within each man that pushes towards action.

This path, in recognition of the energy that must be released, is based on local gatherings of boys and men in games or competitions that are played daily. The games must include physical exertion—with or without contact—that releases heat, adrenaline, and potassium. The release of these components reduces aggressive behavior.

Daily physical exertion is key to lowering conflict. Watching other men in physical competitions initiates the release of the conflict components, but becomes a catalyst for frustration if personal release does not occur. Boys and men who are inactive disturb the energy-release requirement. Inactivity produces alternate "routes" for release that can cause uncontrollable bursts of anger, emotional distress, and illness.

The application of this path has global implications when each small area implements it: local disagreements lessen, regional barriers relax, and conflicts fade. The release of conflict components through daily local gatherings of males participating in games or competitions affects neighborhood groups, corporate management, and government leaders. From young to old, the physical gatherings help the men create a future that is less conflicted.

(This information was originally excluded from the book. Spirit intended it for later publication, but Renee pushed for its inclusion.)

INVESTING IN POTENTIAL

HORRIFIC acts imbalance societies terribly. Their far-reaching effects upset family structures and societal arrangements. The people who perform the horrific acts are permanently scarred, and the people who are their community suffer proportionally.

Conflict breeds conflict breeding more conflict, but why? The natural live-and-let-live formation of society should limit it. Conflict is an aberration. It is not true human nature.

The natural idea-developing, arrangement-building interactivity of people has been misunderstood and relegated to one more thing about human interaction, when in actuality, it IS HOW PEOPLE SHOULD BE INTERACTING!

How People Should be Interacting

In a connected society—one in which the importance of building connections among people is recognized—each person has a responsibility to consider how his or her actions affect the others. Self-care is valued, and so is care of the others.

Talents of each person have value, with each person contributing according to abilities and pace. Natural leaders take leadership roles, understanding that their roles must consider the needs of the societal members. Their power lies in their ability to relate to the youth. The youth have responsibility of caring for the surroundings, and the elders are responsible for tending the surroundings and overseeing daily functioning of the community.

Respect for religious differences prevails. Respect for lifestyle manifestations allows people to express individual temperaments. Respect for difficulties of people born with physical or intellectual limitations is given without pity. Respect for the environment is an everyday occurrence.

The interactions of people—with animals, the land, natural events, and other people—satisfy the need for connections. The interactions join the underlying rhythm of life that pulsates with the flow of blood in each creature's life. The more interactions, the more the rhythm strengthens.

Interactions that leave some feeling betrayed or fearful bring unrest into the picture. The movement away from natural acceptance of others is movement misdirected. The more effort put into living in harmony, the richer the colors of the picture that is created at each moment of life. The constantly-changing, ever-growing picture is meant to be balanced and intertwined.

How People Can Reach Potential

This book has offered explanations for the cycling of contempt and conflict within human existence. Contempt and conflict have become catalysts for distancing from the ideal. They destroy societies and they harm future generations.

Ideal is possible when contempt and conflict are moderated. Events will always occur that enable contempt and conflict to simmer, even boil, but they aren't in control when deliberate actions are taken to ignore them.

Ignoring the feelings that ignite contempt and conflict builds resistance to them and affects the rhythm of life vibrationally. Overcoming negative forces and choosing to bring out compassion pave the way for serenity.

Reaching potential as a society is possible through daily connection to environmental forces (being part of nature, feeling its changes, and protecting it); self-nurturance (creating habits that uplift); group efforts to prevent conflict; personal responsibility to resist self-interest; and gratitude for the gifts of the region and the efforts of society (individual societal members, respectful connection to people who are related, who provide services, and who become close or peripheral acquaintances).

The requirements for reaching potential as a society, which were presented above, can be rewritten with more detail:

Daily connection to environmental forces

- Each day, observe plants and notice their uniqueness: the height and breadth of trees, the colors and shapes of flowers, and the structure and power of leaves.

- Each day, notice the subtle and not so subtle changes in the seasons and smell the changes.

- Each day, nurture elements of nature: outdoor plants, indoor plants, or littered areas.

- Each day, connect to pets or notice animals that are cared for by others or live freely. Marvel at their antics.

- Each day, when you taste nature—through eating fresh fruit or vegetables—taste their connection to the earth and taste their gift of sustenance. The sustenance from the earth is a gift.

Self-nurturance

- Just like an infant, feel your body's basic needs, and as an adult, responsibly provide responses:

  - If your body is thirsty, drink water.

  - If your body is hungry, eat nutritious foods.

  - If your sense of snuggling calls out for closeness, hug a family member or good friend.

- If tiredness demands rest, make rest a priority.

- When demands to rid the body of urine and feces require action, respond and don't ignore the important need to remove waste.

- Stay curious.

- Know that the body needs to move and stay put. If your days are spent in constant motion, add more moments of stillness. If your days are spent being inactive, add intentional movement throughout the day.

- Nurture your talents and desires to create.

- For men: know that your body needs to release energy differently from women. Participate in games or competitions with other men that provide (1) challenges that are physical and mental, (2) reasons to yell and scream, and (3) adrenaline release.

Group efforts to prevent conflict

- Speak out against messages of prejudice.

- Choose leaders who value inclusiveness.

- Stop actions that reflect superiority thinking.

Personal responsibility to resist self-interest

- Regularly practice benevolent thinking: visualize kindness or envisage yourself being compassionate.

- See the turf you traverse as being in your hands to care for. Relate to it as if you are its caregiver, even if you are there temporarily. Help beautify and tend the area—alone or with others.

- Push yourself to be less judgmental of family members, people who are very different from you, and rivals. When judgmental thoughts invade your thinking, switch to thoughts about emptiness. Let the empty visualizations stay in your mind until the judgmental movement passes.

- Treat all service providers with kindness.

Gratitude for the gifts of the region and the efforts of society

- Think about things in your life for which you are grateful. The things can be dear to you, like a beloved person, or mundane, like grocery stores. From time to time, make a list of these things, and be aware of all that is in your life for which you can be grateful.

- Besides treating all service providers with kindness, show them gratitude as well.

- Explore gratitude rituals that instill expressions of thanks. Religions and support groups have such rituals. If established rituals don't appeal to you, create rituals that express your personal gratitude.

- When unwanted events cause despair, open to supportive people and release into the comfort of their connection with you.

How People Can Connect

Dynamic and beating rhythm vibrates endlessly. The rhythm resonates with the movements of each living thing—each blade of grass, each infant, each orangutan, each beetle—and connects them all unseeingly. People live within the rhythm of the connections, just as the other inhabitants of the world do.

The more the living elements are connected, the better the rhythm binds them. The rhythm balances the living without their awareness, and gives them life. The rhythm of the living is sustaining.

The connections that people build with each other, and with the nonhuman elements, resonate in the rhythm. Destructive feelings and actions disrupt the rhythm. Each action performed positively builds the rhythm; each action performed negatively unbalances it.

Of all the living matter in the world, people have the most influence on the rhythm. Our thoughts, decisions, and actions have impact. When we connect with the animals and other creatures in a responsible way; when we connect to our families, friends, acquaintances, community members, and unknown people with desire for camaraderie; when we see the environment as a gift to protect; and when we are open to our soulful guidance, and allow those who depend on us to be soulfully guided, then the rhythm resonates with depth.

When we accept feelings of superiority, or expect to receive what other have and feel resentful, or allow despair to deepen disappointments, or glorify actions that lead to uncontrolled release of harmful destruction, then we allow conflict and contempt to shift the rhythm, and the global rhythm for all living elements is affected.

Descending into conflicts is movement wasted. Energy is best directed towards acceptance, protection, and connection!

NOTES

INDEX

AUTHOR CONNECTION

Renee Rothberg, Energy Guidance Complete author and guide, is the voice of Spiritual Presence through books, articles, blogs, private EGC sessions, and seminars.

Renee was born and raised in Galveston, Texas, and lives in the Galilee of northern Israel. Besides her university degree, she has studied nutrition, kinesiology, aromatherapy, and Libra Method (holistic balance for spine and joints, developed in Israel). Renee is a certified Libra practitioner.

Working with Energy Guidance Complete has enabled Renee to know truths about many topics. The topic of war was hard for her to approach, and Spirit had to push and push her to write this book.

Renee's blog is available on her website: www.energy-guidance-complete.com